Wild West Shows

Wild West Shows

Rough Riders and Sure Shots

by Judy Alter

A First Book

FRANKLIN WATTS

A DIVISION OF GROLIER PUBLISHING

New York   London   Hong Kong   Sydney
Danbury, Connecticut

Photographs ©: Archive Photos: 48, 49; Brown Brothers: 2, 10, 25, 30, 33, 41, 42, 45; Buffalo Bill Historical Center, Cody, WY: 38, 39 (Gift of Carl Downing), 46, 57; Corbis-Bettmann: 9, 13, 18, 19, 29, 52, 54; Culver Pictures: 20, 21, 36, 37; Denver Public Library, Western History Department: 23; North Wind Picture Archives: 13, 14; UPI/Corbis-Bettmann: 26, 51.

Library of Congress Cataloging-in-Publication Data

Alter, Judy, 1938–
    Wild West shows : rough riders and sure shots / Judy Alter.
        p. cm. — (A First book)
    Includes bibliographical references and index.
    Summary: Describes the rise and fall of Wild West shows and discusses the entertainment's legendary characters, including Buffalo Bill, Annie Oakley, and Pawnee Bill.
    ISBN 0-531-20274-7 (lib.bdg.)   0-531-15875-6 (pbk.)
    1. Wild west shows—Juvenile literature. [1. Wild west shows.
2. West (U.S.)—History.] I. Title. II. Series.
    GV1833.A48 1997
    791.8'4—dc20   96-41099
                                                CIP
                                                AC

CONTENTS

One

A SHOWMAN NAMED BUFFALO BILL

"Ladies and gentlemen, I have the honor of introducing to your attention a man whose record as a servant of the government, whose skill and daring as a frontiersman, whose place in history as the chief of scouts of the United States Army, . . . whose name as one of the avengers of the lamented Custer, and whose adherence throughout an eventful life to his chosen principle of 'true to friend and foe,' have made him well and popularly known throughout the world. . . . The honorable William F. Cody, 'Buffalo Bill!' "

Buffalo Bill looked the part of a legendary man of the Wild West. He wore his hair shoulder length, matched by a mustache and goatee, and he was clad in buckskin. In his later years, his hair and goatee turned white and he wore white buckskin. At the announcer's introduction, he would ride a prancing horse into the ring and proclaim loudly, "Wild West, are you ready? Go!" Thus began thousands of Wild West performances from 1883 until almost World War I, which began in 1914. Wild West shows cannot be studied without a close look at Buffalo Bill, who scorned the term "show," calling his exhibitions simply "Buffalo Bill's Wild West."

Born in 1846 in Iowa, William F. Cody grew up in Kansas. At the age of eleven, he went to work for a freighting firm and later rode for the Pony Express. Bill Cody met such legendary mountain men as Jim Bridger and Kit Carson at Fort Laramie and fought Native Americans—he would have called them Indians—with frontiersman Wild Bill Hickok. The Civil War was in its last years when Bill Cody turned eighteen in 1864 and he enlisted in the Seventh Kansas Voluntary Cavalry.

A master showman, William F. Cody is credited with popularizing the Wild West show.

After the war, Bill Cody worked as a scout and guide in the West. He earned the nickname "Buffalo Bill" after being hired to supply buffalo meat to crews working on the Union Pacific Railroad. Although at least a dozen men across the West had the same nickname, none of them ever achieved Cody's fame. General Philip H. Sheridan then hired Buffalo Bill to report on the activities and whereabouts of Indian tribes as chief of scouts for the Fifth U.S. Cavalry. He was with the cavalry four years, participating in sixteen Indian fights.

In 1872, Buffalo Bill guided a special group of tourists, which included the Grand Duke Alexis of Russia, the Earl of Dunraven from England, and the editor of the *New York Herald*, on a hunt. In 1876, he was with the Fifth Cavalry at the Battle at Warbonnet Creek, where he killed a Cheyenne named Yellow Hair, sometimes also called Yellow Hand. This victory was called "the first scalp for Custer," in retaliation for the defeat and death of General George A. Custer earlier that year in Wyoming at the Battle of Little Bighorn.

During these years, a man named Edward Z. C. Judson was writing books that dramatized episodes in the American West under the pen name Ned Buntline. These

Frontiersman Buffalo Bill learned about the Wild West firsthand.

kinds of books, called dime novels because they sold for ten cents, might be compared to today's paperbacks displayed on racks in grocery stores and airports. Buntline made Buffalo Bill the hero of several dime novels, including a sensationalized version of the hunt with Grand Duke Alexis. He even persuaded Buffalo Bill to appear onstage in melodramatic reenactments of his adventures.

Buffalo Bill eventually broke with Buntline, but he remained in **vaudeville** for eleven winter seasons, hunting and guiding during the summers. Buffalo Bill's vaudeville experience no doubt contributed to his instinct for showmanship and his craving for applause. Buntline deserves credit for creating a national audience for Buffalo Bill and readying the country for Buffalo Bill's Wild West.

Buffalo Bill is generally acknowledged as the creator of the Wild West show. In 1882, he accepted the challenge to plan a "blowout" in his hometown of North Platte, Nebraska. In this show, cowboys would compete for prizes donated by local businessmen in riding, roping, and shooting events. Buffalo Bill expected, at the most, one hundred entrants; he attracted a thousand cowboys.

Buffalo Bill, shown here in a cover illustration catching an outlaw, was the hero of many popular dime novels.

The BUFFALO BILL STORIES

Devoted To Far West Life

BUFFALO BILL AND THE SILK LASSO

OR PAWNEE BILL'S MASQUERADE

BY THE AUTHOR OF "BUFFALO BILL"

STREET & SMITH
PUBLISHERS
NEW YORK

Buffalo Bill's outdoor show in North Platte included buffalo hunting.

The event in North Platte was not original. Many towns still claim the distinction of having held the first rodeo, and by 1882, cowboy competitions were a popular way to celebrate Independence Day in the West. Buffalo Bill, however, added two new things to his competition: a demonstration of his methods of killing buffalo and a marksmanship presentation. He had taken part of his vaudeville show and turned it into an outdoor exhibition.

The show Buffalo Bill produced in North Platte owes much to the outdoor-arena tradition of traveling circuses, common throughout America at that time. "The Old Glory Blowout," as Buffalo Bill called the show, was such a success that he decided to take it on the road the next year.

At this point, the difference between rodeos and Wild West shows

becomes important. What Buffalo Bill presented in North Platte was primarily a rodeo, an event in which cowboys paid an entry fee to compete for prizes. A Wild West show, on the other hand, is professional entertainment, an exhibition by paid performers presenting scenes associated with the American frontier. The show that Buffalo Bill took on the road was more entertainment than competition.

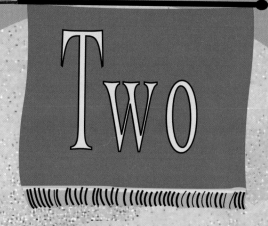

TWO

"THE MOST OVERWHELMINGLY THRILLING SPECTACLE"

For his traveling show, Buffalo Bill added several new attractions. The acts included a staged attack on the Deadwood Stage, a Pony Express ride, a demonstration in which cowboys rode wild Texas steers, and a dramatization of an Indian attack on a pioneer log cabin.

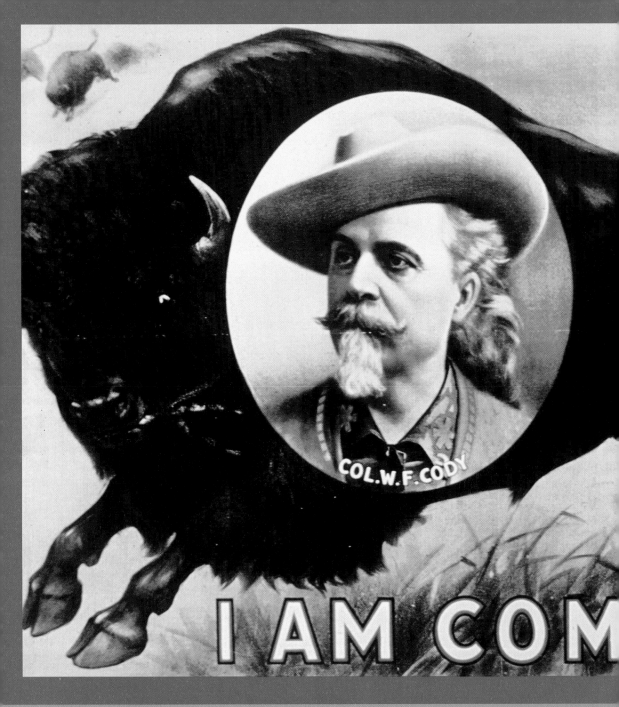

This Buffalo Bill's Wild West poster promotes the show in advance of its arrival.

Buffalo Bill's early advertising set a standard for later Wild West shows. Advance men went into a town ahead of the show and covered the city with posters advertising the "grandest, most realistic and overwhelmingly thrilling spectacle ever seen." They gave out handbills, or **heralds**, printed on both sides of cheap paper called "circus" paper.

The show's advance men occasionally distributed a newspaper called a **courier**. These newspapers, eight or sixteen pages long, were cut out in the shape of a buffalo head or Buffalo Bill himself sometimes. For several years, Buffalo Bill's show produced

Wild West shows often began with a parade through town.

an annual courier titled *Rough Rider*. The colorful publication was filled with information about the show and its features.

But the **billboard** is the advertising most associated with these shows. Billboards were large sheets of paper plastered on almost any surface. The largest billboard, called a twenty-four sheet, was twenty-four times the size of an average piece of paper. An advance man would piece a twenty-four sheet together like a jigsaw puzzle using glue and paste it on the sides of barns, outhouses, and fences. Farmers were glad to see billboards on their barns because the papers added a little protection to a building and, more important, the usual payment was free tickets to the show.

These colorful posters, often done by well-known artists, were filled with scenes of action: Buffalo Bill on a prancing horse, Indians doing a dance around a fire, or

a desperate battle between settlers and Indians. One of the
most famous billboards showed King Edward VII of England
greeting a young Indian boy.

When the show hit a new town, it began with a
parade, which was designed to interest townspeople in
the upcoming performance. In small communities, the
parade was no doubt a welcome and exciting event.

Some people, however, believed that the performers in Wild West shows were wicked and idle. Each show required a great number of low-paid workers to care for the animals and put up the tents. The latter, called roustabouts, were often rough in manners and talk, which led to further distrust of the Wild West show. And no matter how honest the show's operation, gamblers usually followed the show from town to town—and they were not always honest. Show people developed their own term for the unfair practices of these gamblers: grift. Many shows hired detectives to keep their grounds free of these questionable people and activities.

That first year, Buffalo Bill's three-hour show was not an overwhelming success. Profits were low, and Buffalo Bill broke with two of his early partners, William "Doc" Carver, an expert marksman, and Adam Bogardus. Both men would go on to have shows of their own.

In the mid-1880s, Buffalo Bill added to the show the famous Sioux chief, Sitting Bull, who had taken part in Custer's defeat at the Battle of Little Bighorn. Then he added Annie Oakley, an unknown who could shoot with an accuracy no one had ever dreamed of—especially when a girl was the marksman!

Sioux chief Sitting Bull and Buffalo Bill pose together in this 1885 photograph.

Annie Oakley was not a westerner. Born Phoebe Anne Moses, she grew up in the woods of Ohio. She was famous for providing head-shot birds for local hotels to serve their guests. Unlike others at the time, Annie Oakley killed a bird by shooting it in the head. She did not scatter birdshot—the small pellets that fill the shell—through the edible portions of the bird, which reduced its value on a fancy menu.

By the 1880s, Annie Oakley and her husband Frank Butler were touring as sharpshooters with the Sells Circus. When the show closed in 1885, they found themselves abandoned in New Orleans, Louisiana, and hired on with Buffalo Bill, who was at first reluctant to hire a woman sharpshooter. He put Oakley on trial—and immediately hired her when he saw what she could do with a rifle and a shotgun. Butler withdrew from competition to promote his wife's career. Annie Oakley became the greatest of the Wild West stars, next to Buffalo Bill himself. The newspapers called her "America's Sweetheart." Sitting Bull dubbed her "Little Sure Shot."

Annie Oakley customarily had the second spot on the program. Some say it was to help the women in the audience get accustomed to the sound of gunfire before Buffalo Bill's marksmanship demonstrations later in the show.

Sharpshooter Annie Oakley earned her fame in Wild West shows.

Apparently, gunfire was less likely to offend if a woman did the shooting. Annie Oakley was prim, proper, and barely 5 feet (1.5 m) tall. Almost childlike, she charmed audiences as she skipped onto the stage. But she impressed everyone with her marksmanship. She could shoot unlimited numbers of clay pigeons, 943 out of 1,000 glass balls, and 4,772 out of 5,000 targets with a rifle in nine hours. Her most famous trick was splitting a playing card

Shooting targets while she balanced on the back of a galloping horse was Annie Oakley's specialty.

edgewise. And she once shot a cigarette out of the mouth of a European prince.

During the 1880s, Buffalo Bill took on a man named Nate Salsbury as his managing partner. Salsbury had twelve years experience with his own troupe, The Troubadours, and had been interested in Buffalo Bill's show since its beginnings. His job was to make up for Buffalo Bill's lack of business sense, which led him to fall for almost every investment scheme that came his way. Salsbury also put limits on Buffalo Bill's generosity, which often prompted him to give away profits from the show.

Buffalo Bill and Salsbury's first big triumph together was a scene added for a winter show in Madison Square Garden in 1886 and 1887. The production, called "The Drama of Civilization," was hailed for its realistic effects, including a "Kansas cyclone," produced with steam-powered fans and lots of dead leaves. Buffalo Bill also added a scene reenacting Custer's death at the Battle of Little Bighorn.

Three

ROUGH RIDERS
IN EUROPE

In 1887, Buffalo Bill and Nate Salsbury were invited to take their show to England as part of Queen Victoria's Golden Jubilee celebration. They sailed with 180 horses, eighteen buffalo, ten elk, ten mules, five Texas steers, four donkeys, and two deer. More than two hundred people were in the troupe, almost half of whom were Native Americans.

Among the acts Buffalo Bill added to the British version of the show was a scene featuring a prairie fire about to engulf an emigrant wagon train. The tour was triumphant and as many as fifty thousand people attended the daily performances. Royalty and commoners alike were fascinated.

In this cartoon, Buffalo Bill meets the Pope during his European tour.

Buffalo Bill's Wild West returned to America after its triumphant tour. Within two years, the show was back in Europe, this time for a tour that would last four years. Annie Oakley, who had briefly left to join another troupe, was back, and they toured France, Italy, Germany, Austria, and Spain, where a typhoid epidemic took the lives of several performers and limited audience turnout.

On a brief trip back to the United States during this extended European tour, Buffalo Bill was called by General Nelson A. Miles to deal with Wovoka and the Ghost Dance religious movement. Wovoka had arisen among the Plains Indians as their new savior and was threatening an uprising. The plan was for Buffalo Bill to work for peace with his old friend Sitting Bull, but he arrived in Nebraska too late. When Indian police tried to arrest Sitting Bull, the chief was shot to death. The Battle of Wounded Knee followed, and Buffalo Bill served as a brigadier general in the Nebraska state troops.

Meanwhile, back in Europe, Salsbury was planning an addition to the show that would include horsemen of all nations: German and English soldiers, Argentinian gauchos, Mexican vaqueros, and Russian cavalrymen called cossacks. Called "Congress of Rough Riders of the

These Mexican cowboys, called vaqueros, performed with Buffalo Bill's Wild West.

World," it was an instant success. Buffalo Bill, back in Europe for the performance, presumably approved the new direction of the show. In 1891, members of Africa's Zulu tribe and performing elephants were added to the lineup. Clearly, the show was moving away from its Wild West origins.

The peak of success for the Buffalo Bill show came in the United States in 1893, when the troupe performed at the World's Columbian Exposition in Chicago, Illinois. The show was not part of the exposition, nor was it allowed inside the gates. Nate Salsbury, however, had leased a lot near the main entrance, and most of the 27 million exposition visitors also attended Buffalo Bill's Wild West and Congress of Rough Riders. The show is said to have grossed one million dollars, a staggering sum of money for the time.

With performers such as these acrobats, Buffalo Bill's show departed from its roots in the Wild West.

Four

CHANGES IN COMPETITION

By 1894, Buffalo Bill's Wild West was in debt again and Nate Salsbury, seriously ill, left, never to return. After complicated negotiations, James Bailey of the famed Barnum & Bailey Circus took control. In exchange for a share in the show, Bailey was to provide the show's transportation and local expenses.

The next year, Bailey sent the show over 9,000 miles

(14,485 km) to do 131 stands in 199 days. The number of one-day shows was hard on the animals and performers. Buffalo Bill was constantly working to update the show and add new acts. Some sources even say the notorious western woman Calamity Jane once appeared in the show.

Yet the show's fortunes continued to fall. A 1901 train wreck killed 110 horses and injured Annie Oakley, who never again worked for Buffalo Bill. In 1902, Buffalo Bill's Wild West went on its last European tour. Over the next four years, the show played in England, France, Austria, Hungary, Germany, and Belgium. The show made enough money to allow Buffalo Bill to donate five thousand dollars to the survivors of the eruption of Italy's Mount Vesuvius and one thousand dollars to San Francisco's earthquake and fire relief. Near the end of the tour, an epidemic of a contagious and often fatal disease called glanders killed two hundred of the troupe's horses.

To complicate the show's fortunes further, popular interest in the Wild West was fading by the turn of the century. And, encouraged by Buffalo Bill's success at the Columbian Exposition in 1893, several major and even more minor companies had started up Wild West shows of their own to compete with Buffalo Bill's.

Buffalo Bill had two major competitors, and he was destined to join each of them in the early years of this cen-

This poster advertises a Buffalo Bill show featuring flags and horsemen from around the world.

tury. They were the "Pawnee Bill Historical Wild West Exhibition and Indian Encampment" and the "Miller Brothers 101 Ranch Real Wild West" show.

Gordon W. Lillie, better known as Pawnee Bill, started

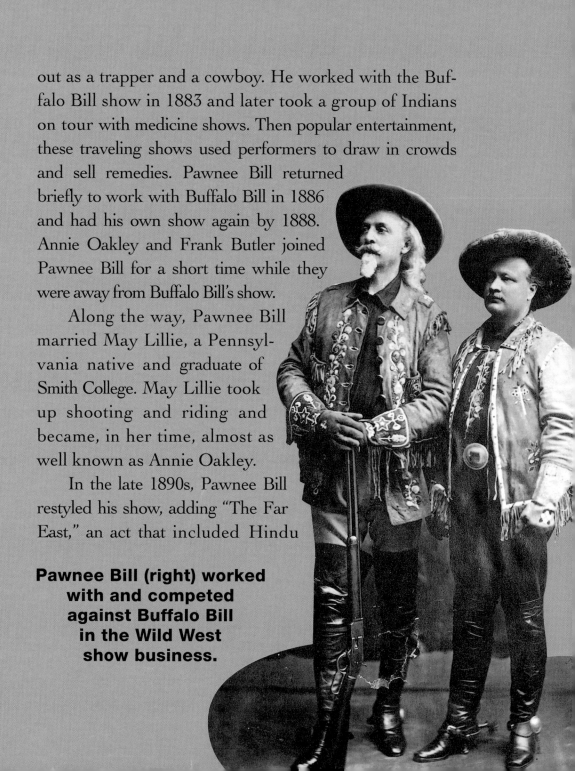

out as a trapper and a cowboy. He worked with the Buffalo Bill show in 1883 and later took a group of Indians on tour with medicine shows. Then popular entertainment, these traveling shows used performers to draw in crowds and sell remedies. Pawnee Bill returned briefly to work with Buffalo Bill in 1886 and had his own show again by 1888. Annie Oakley and Frank Butler joined Pawnee Bill for a short time while they were away from Buffalo Bill's show.

Along the way, Pawnee Bill married May Lillie, a Pennsylvania native and graduate of Smith College. May Lillie took up shooting and riding and became, in her time, almost as well known as Annie Oakley.

In the late 1890s, Pawnee Bill restyled his show, adding "The Far East," an act that included Hindu

Pawnee Bill (right) worked with and competed against Buffalo Bill in the Wild West show business.

magicians, Senegalese dancers, Madagascar oxen cavalry, and Chinese and Japanese cavalry. A far cry from the real Wild West, it indicated the public's declining interest in the American West.

The Pawnee Bill show soon merged with Buffalo Bill's. After James Bailey died, his heirs made a deal to sell their share of Buffalo Bill's Wild West to Pawnee Bill. At first, Buffalo Bill would not agree to sharing equal billing with his former employee and rival. However, without the money to buy out Bailey's heirs, Buffalo Bill had little choice. The two showmen finally settled on a name: "Buffalo Bill's Wild West Combined with Pawnee Bill's Far East." Most people called it "The Two Bills Show."

Sensing the public's interest in things military, Buffalo Bill added military acts to the new show. They

ETHNOLOGICAL CONGRESS
SKILL of ALL NATIONS.

"The Two Bills Show" boasted a variety of acts from several countries.

included a Gatling machine-gun demonstration and "The Battle of San Juan Hill," a reenactment of Theodore Roosevelt's famous 1898 charge up a Puerto Rican hill during the Spanish-American War.

In 1909, Buffalo Bill and Pawnee Bill toured the United States with a modernized show that advertised automobiles and featured a locomotive that puffed black smoke and had electric headlights. New features also included a game on horseback played with a 5-foot (1.5-m) ball, "The Great Train Hold-Up," and horses trained in the intricate steps of the Spanish riding school. Guided by a rider, the horses would lie down and roll over, bow to the audience, and follow a complicated dance pattern. In spite of these and other new acts, the Two Bills show lost money.

Five

FAREWELL AND GOODBYE

In 1910, Buffalo Bill staged a series of "Farewell Exhibitions." When he cried "This farewell visit will be my last 'Hail and Farewell' in the saddle to you," people wept. The farewells went on through 1912. Profits for the show continued to slide.

Finally, the bankrupt show was sold at auction to Sells-Floto Circus. Buffalo Bill was forced to spend the

1914–1915 season traveling with the circus. By October 1915, Buffalo Bill could boast that he had never missed a performance, and he had cleared his debt to the owners of Sells-Floto.

By 1910, the Miller Brothers 101 Ranch Real Wild West show was emerging as a serious competitor. The Miller 101 was an Oklahoma ranch run by three bachelor brothers named Joseph, Zack, and George Miller. The Miller 101 was one of a few entirely self-sufficient ranches. The Millers had their own vegetable gardens, fruit orchards, slaughterhouse, packing plant, dairy, tannery, cannery, saddle shop, laundry, company store, and

To clear himself of debt, Buffalo Bill traveled with the Sells-Floto Circus for one season.

trading post. After oil was discovered on the property, the Millers also had a refinery and filling station.

The Miller brothers got into the Wild West business in 1906 when they staged a round-up for a convention of the National Editorial Association. The Miller brothers were eager to show this group of editors, largely from the East Coast, what the real West was like. The show featured Apache chief Geronimo, who was brought from Fort Sill for one last buffalo hunt, and roper Lucille Mulhall, from a neighboring ranch.

Popularly called the "first cowgirl," Lucille Mulhall was to roping what Annie Oakley was to shooting. Later in her career, Mulhall would rope eight men riding abreast and beat out most men in roping competitions.

The Millers took their show east to Chicago in 1912 and then to Brighton Beach near New York City. They mostly used local talent from their own ranch in Oklahoma, but some famous names got their start with the Miller show. Singing cowboy Tom Mix began as a Miller hand. Bill Pickett, the African-American cowboy famous for inventing steer wrestling, or bulldogging, worked for the Miller 101 nearly all his life.

A true cowboy, Zack Miller of the Miller 101 Ranch Real Wild West show stands with his horse in front of his family's ranch.

The most famous Miller talent, however, was cowboy-humorist-performer Will Rogers. Rogers shot to fame during a Miller show in Madison Square Garden when Lucille Mulhall (or, according to some, Tom Mix) came up with an empty loop during a steer-roping act. Deciding it was safer in the stands, the steer crashed its way into the audience. When Mulhall's second loop also came up empty, Rogers roped the runaway steer and saved the day. From there, he went on to national fame.

The Miller 101 added yet a new dimension to the Wild West show with acts depicting Civil War battleships the *Monitor* and the *Merrimack*, Pocahontas and Captain John Smith, and Colonel Francis Ferrari's wild animals. The Millers traveled nationally and in 1914, following Buffalo Bill's example, took their show to England.

Six months of triumph for the Miller 101 were followed by disaster. At the outbreak of World War I, the British government commandeered all horses, including those in the show. Zack Miller lost all but six trick horses and the show returned home.

Buffalo Bill began touring with a show called "Buffalo Bill (Himself) and the 101 Ranch Wild West, Combined with the Military Preparedness Pageant." As World

Popular performer and humorist Will Rogers got his start in Wild West shows.

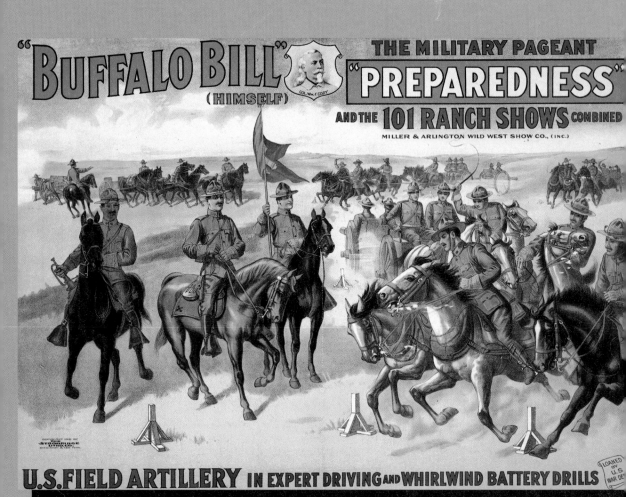

War I raged in Europe and threatened the United States, military preparedness was on everyone's minds. Acts in the new show included "Regular Members of the U.S. Cavalry in Military Exercises, Athletic Sports, and Horse-

During World War I, audiences attended Wild West shows with a military theme.

manship," "U.S. Artillery Drill," and "Reproduction of the Battle of Columbus, New Mexico, showing Villa's Attack." (Mexican revolutionary Pancho Villa had attacked the New Mexico town in early 1916.)

The show toured through November 1916. Buffalo Bill died in Denver, Colorado, on January 10, 1917. The Miller show hung on for one more year, but by 1918, no major Wild West shows were touring the country.

After World War I, the acts and stars returned but in different ways. During the war, the stars had often earned their fame elsewhere, particularly in Hollywood horse operas. Celebrities such as Ken Maynard and Tom Mix put together short-lived shows. Instead of being a show on its own, the Wild West spectacle was often just a small part of a touring circus or carnival. Finally, other forms of entertainment such as film and radio took over the presentation of the Wild West. Why was it necessary to go see Buffalo Bill when you could stay home and listen to the adventures of the Lone Ranger on the radio?

The Miller 101 returned to the show circuit in 1925, adding elk, buffalo, elephants, and camels to the bill. The show also featured award-winning Texas trick-rider Tad Lucas and well-known daredevil cowboy Milt Hinkle.

Wild West shows contributed greatly to the growing popularity of rodeos.

"Suicide" Ted Elder also did the Roman ride, standing astride two racing horses with one foot in each saddle. In a spectacular feat, he sometimes stood with two more horses between the two on which he balanced.

By 1931, following the death of two of the three Miller brothers, the Miller 101 was reduced to bankruptcy, and the family lost the Oklahoma ranch. With show business in his blood, Zack Miller continued to work in the outdoor exhibition business in one form or another for the next twenty years.

Finally, the Wild West show was overtaken by a sudden rise in the popularity of rodeo. Rodeo has, in fact, been called the legitimate offspring of the Wild West show. The standard rodeos—Frontier Days in Cheyenne, Wyoming; the Calgary Stampede in Alberta, Canada; and the Oregon Round-Up in Pendleton—had been in operation for years. But after World War I, these competitions replaced the Wild West shows, incorporating acts from the shows into their programs.

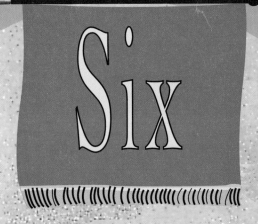

Six

WOMEN AND INDIANS ONSTAGE

In its heyday, the Wild West show offered unusual employment opportunities for women and a chance to escape the reservations for many Native Americans. Due in part to the popular stage show *Annie Get Your Gun*, ace markswoman Annie Oakley remains familiar to millions of Americans. Annie Oakley has become a beloved and permanent figure in American folklore, but she was by no means the only woman to star in these shows.

Stars such as Lucille Mulhall, Tad Lucas, and May Lillie also earned names for themselves. Countless other women rode bucking broncs, roped wild steers, and entered relay races in various Wild West shows. They also risked their lives in trick and fancy riding.

At the peak of the Wild West show, at a time when women's lives were usually limited to home, church, and family, female performers defied tradition to join traveling Wild West shows. They also managed to raise families on the road, often traveling with their husbands.

Many women spent much of their lives touring and performing in Wild West shows.

It is interesting that so many of the women in Wild West shows acted in the dramatic scenes portraying defenseless women. Although these performers had moved beyond typical female roles in their personal lives, onstage they played the threatened housewife at the cabin under attack and the frightened female on the stagecoach about to be robbed.

For many Native Americans, the shows offered an escape from the confinement of the reservation and an opportunity to travel. Chiefs like Sitting Bull who traveled with the shows became celebrities and enjoyed fame and attention during the run of the show.

The Native American women in Wild West shows almost never achieved stardom and were confined to playing some version of a traditional Indian woman. They were most often seen in melodramatic capture scenes as the torturers of white captives. The Native American men who did not play chiefs were nameless in numerous attack scenes and often appeared as the "bad guys."

The Wild West shows did, however, show Indian life as more than one long battle with invading settlers.

In this typical Wild West show act, Buffalo Bill saves a helpless woman from Indians on the attack.

53

Buffalo Bill sits with some of the Native American men, women, and children who were part of his troupe.

Various scenes attempted to portray life in the villages of the Plains Indians. These people were shown to be superb horsemen, skilled hunters, and real people, not merely faceless, warring enemies.

Seven

LEGACY OF THE WILD WEST SHOW

Buffalo Bill died in debt, a victim of his spend-thrift ways. Although he earned great sums during his life in show business, he spent his profits unwisely. Buffalo Bill invested in the development of the town of Cody, Wyoming, complete with the Hotel Irma (named after his daughter), an Arizona mining and milling company that fleeced him of half a million dollars, a patent medicine scheme, and a plan to colonize Mexico.

Buffalo Bill, however, is not remembered for his financial failures. The making of the cowboy hero may well be Buffalo Bill's most important accomplishment. Before Buffalo Bill's Wild West show, cowboys were considered ruffians and desperadoes, or bandits, and the term "hired man on horseback" was an insult. After Buffalo Bill brought the cowboy (and Indian and soldier) onstage, the cowboy hero became part of the great myth of the American West.

Wild West shows offered many myths about the American West. They offered audiences a variety of romanticized stories of frontier life: spectacular fights between Indians and frontiersmen who always triumphed; scenes of wagon trains circling up and fierce, painted Indian warriors fleeing in howling defeat; and marksmanship demonstrations carried out by handsome, well-dressed cowboys (and cowgirls) who almost always hit their targets.

The American West that Buffalo Bill portrayed onstage in turn gave rise to a flood of western culture. That culture includes movies featuring stars from John

Buffalo Bill and the Wild West show helped shape our image of the American West.

Wayne to Clint Eastwood, television shows from *Bonanza* and *Gunsmoke* to *Dr. Quinn, Medicine Woman*, and a publishing industry that produces novels commonly called westerns or "shoot-'em ups." Today, businesses of all kinds capitalize on the western theme to sell products ranging from salad dressing to restaurant dinners.

Buffalo Bill and the Wild West show brought frontier life to the stage for audiences that had almost no firsthand knowledge of the American West. Not merely entertainment, the Wild West show made lasting contributions to our picture of the American West.

WILD WEST SHOW TERMS

billboard—a smooth surface such as a wall or fence covered with posters to advertise traveling shows

clay pigeon—a disk of baked clay hurled into the air from a trap as a target for a sharpshooter to hit

courier—an elaborately illustrated newspaper to advertise traveling shows such as Buffalo Bill's Wild West, which printed the popular courier *Rough Rider*

gaucho—a cowboy of the South American plains

heralds—two-sided announcements printed on cheap, brightly colored paper and distributed by hand to advertise traveling shows

horse opera—a television play, radio show, novel, or movie, usually presented with much drama, about Indians, cowboys, gunmen, and prospectors in the Wild West

vaquero—a Mexican cowboy

vaudeville—a kind of theatrical show consisting of several varied acts such as dancing, singing, and comedy

Wild West—a term for the western United States from the end of Civil War in 1865 to the turn of the century; it refers to the lawlessness of the time.

FOR FURTHER READING

Alter, Judith. *Women of the Old West*. New York: Franklin Watts, 1989.

Black, Sheila. *Sitting Bull*. Morristown, N.J.: Silver Burdett, 1989.

Buntline, Ned. *Buffalo Bill: His Adventures in the West*. Salem, N.H.: Ayer, 1974.

Davidson, Mary R. *Buffalo Bill: Wild West Showman*. New York: Chelsea House, 1993.

Freedman, Russell. *Cowboys of the Wild West*. Boston: Houghton Mifflin, 1990.

Graves, Charles P. *Annie Oakley: The Shooting Star*. New York: Chelsea House, 1991.

Green, Carl R., and William R. Sanford. *Wild Bill Hickok*. New York: Enslow, 1992.

INDEX

Page numbers in *italics* indicate illustrations.

About the Author

Judy Alter is the author of several books for children, including *Women of the Old West*, *The Comanches*, *Rodeos: The Greatest Show on Dirt*, and *Beauty Pageants: Tiaras, Roses, and Runways* for Franklin Watts. She is the director of Texas Christian University Press, which publishes literature and history of Texas and the American West. Ms. Alter lives in Fort Worth, Texas.